EMMANUEL JOSEPH

The Pantheon of Play, How AI and Mythology Are Revolutionizing Athletic Excellence

Copyright © 2025 by Emmanuel Joseph

All rights reserved. No part of this publication may be reproduced, stored or transmitted in any form or by any means, electronic, mechanical, photocopying, recording, scanning, or otherwise without written permission from the publisher. It is illegal to copy this book, post it to a website, or distribute it by any other means without permission.

First edition

This book was professionally typeset on Reedsy. Find out more at reedsy.com

Contents

1	Chapter 1: Genesis of the Game	1
2	Chapter 2: The Olympian Data Gods	3
3	Chapter 3: Titans of Training	5
4	Chapter 4: Mythical Performance Enhancements	7
5	Chapter 5: Strategy from the Stars	9
6	Chapter 6: The Hero's Health Journey	11
7	Chapter 7: Fan Engagement: A New Pantheon	13
8	Chapter 8: The Alchemy of AI in Sports Economics	15
9	Chapter 9: Ethical Dimensions of AI in Sports	17
10	Chapter 10: The Future: Beyond the Horizons of Myth	19
11	Chapter 11: The Pantheon's Legacy	21
12	Chapter 14: The Muse of Innovation	23

1

Chapter 1: Genesis of the Game

The convergence of artificial intelligence and ancient mythology is breathing new life into the world of athletics. It's as though the gods of old have descended, bringing their otherworldly prowess and wisdom to contemporary sports. With AI's unprecedented ability to analyze, predict, and simulate, athletes are transcending human limitations, mirroring the legendary feats of Hercules or Achilles. This chapter delves into the birth of this modern alchemy, examining how the interplay between technology and mythological symbolism is reshaping the landscape of athletic excellence.

At the dawn of this technological revolution, AI emerged as a formidable force in sports, akin to the mythical Prometheus, who brought fire to humanity. Just as Prometheus' gift revolutionized human civilization, AI is transforming the realm of sports. The incorporation of machine learning algorithms and data analytics into training and performance monitoring has allowed athletes to push beyond their perceived limits. This synergy between man and machine is akin to the mythic partnerships between gods and mortals, where divine intervention enabled heroes to achieve extraordinary feats.

From the very beginning, the parallels between AI and mythology have been striking. Consider the ancient tales where divine beings bestowed gifts of strength, speed, and skill upon their chosen champions. Today, AI plays a similar role, offering athletes unparalleled insights into their own capabilities and potential. By analyzing vast amounts of data, AI provides a level of understanding that was once the exclusive domain of the divine. This chapter will explore how AI's analytical prowess is akin to the all-seeing eyes of the gods, offering athletes the guidance and knowledge they need to excel.

As we journey through this chapter, we will uncover the myriad ways in which AI is revolutionizing the world of sports. From personalized training regimens to injury prevention strategies, AI's impact is profound and far-reaching. By drawing on the rich tapestry of mythology, we can better understand the significance of these advancements and appreciate the transformative power of this modern-day alchemy. Through this exploration, we will see how the integration of AI and mythology is not only revolutionizing athletic excellence but also enriching our understanding of the human spirit and its boundless potential.

2

Chapter 2: The Olympian Data Gods

In the era of big data, AI acts as the modern Oracle of Delphi, providing insights that were once the domain of divine prophecy. Coaches and athletes now rely on complex algorithms to understand performance metrics and health indicators. This chapter explores the reverence athletes and teams show for data analytics, akin to the veneration of deities. The meticulous process of harnessing this data to predict outcomes, prevent injuries, and optimize training regimens is likened to ancient rituals, where knowledge and foresight were paramount.

Athletes today look to AI for guidance much like ancient civilizations looked to their gods for wisdom. With vast amounts of data at its disposal, AI can analyze every aspect of an athlete's performance, from physical exertion levels to biomechanical efficiency. This divine-like oversight allows for unparalleled precision in training and competition strategies. By understanding these metrics, athletes can fine-tune their routines to achieve optimal performance, akin to the divine perfection sought by mythological heroes.

The role of AI in sports analytics is multifaceted. It not only tracks and records data but also interprets it to provide actionable insights. For instance, wearable technology embedded with AI can monitor an athlete's vitals in real-time, alerting them to any signs of potential injury or fatigue. This proactive approach to health management is reminiscent of the ancient gods' protective vigilance over their favored mortals. By intervening before harm befalls an athlete, AI serves as a guardian, ensuring their well-being and longevity in their sport.

Furthermore, AI's predictive capabilities have transformed the way teams strategize and compete. Through advanced algorithms, AI can simulate countless scenarios, offering coaches a glimpse into possible outcomes and helping them make informed decisions. This predictive power is akin to the prophetic abilities of mythological figures, who could foresee and influence future events. As a result, teams can develop more effective game plans and adapt to changing circumstances with a level of foresight that was once unimaginable.

3

Chapter 3: Titans of Training

Training methodologies have evolved dramatically with AI, transforming ordinary mortals into athletic titans. Using personalized AI-driven programs, athletes can achieve peak performance levels previously thought unattainable. These advancements are reminiscent of the epic quests of myth, where heroes undergo rigorous trials to unlock their full potential. This chapter provides an in-depth look at how AI tailors training to individual needs, ensuring that each athlete can embark on their own heroic journey toward excellence.

The personalization of training programs through AI is a game-changer. By analyzing an athlete's strengths, weaknesses, and unique physical attributes, AI can create a customized regimen that maximizes their potential. This tailored approach is akin to the bespoke trials faced by mythological heroes, each designed to push them to their limits and beyond. Through AI-driven training, athletes can refine their skills, build endurance, and enhance their overall performance in ways that were previously unimaginable.

AI also brings a level of precision to training that mirrors the meticulous craftsmanship of ancient artisans. By continuously monitoring an athlete's progress and adjusting their program in real-time, AI ensures that every aspect of their training is optimized for success. This dynamic adaptability is akin to the evolving challenges faced by heroes on their epic journeys, requiring them to adapt and overcome. As a result, athletes can achieve a level of excellence that rivals the legendary feats of myth.

Moreover, AI-driven training programs offer a holistic approach to athletic development. Beyond physical conditioning, these programs also address mental resilience and strategic thinking. By incorporating psychological and cognitive training, AI helps athletes develop the mental fortitude needed to succeed in high-pressure situations. This comprehensive approach is reminiscent of the multifaceted trials faced by mythological heroes, who had to demonstrate not only physical prowess but also wisdom and courage.

4

Chapter 4: Mythical Performance Enhancements

Performance enhancement has taken on a mythical dimension, with AI technologies pushing the boundaries of human capability. From wearable tech to biomechanical analysis, athletes are equipped with tools that seem to defy natural limits. This chapter examines the integration of AI in gear and apparel, drawing parallels with legendary artifacts like Hermes' winged sandals or Athena's shield. The narrative explores how these innovations are not just augmentations but extensions of the athlete's very essence.

Wearable technology, embedded with AI, has become an essential part of an athlete's arsenal. These devices monitor a wide range of physiological metrics, providing real-time feedback that helps athletes optimize their performance. This level of insight and control is akin to the divine gifts bestowed upon mythological heroes, granting them extraordinary abilities. By leveraging AI, athletes can achieve feats that were once considered impossible, pushing the boundaries of human potential.

Biomechanical analysis, powered by AI, offers a deeper understanding of an athlete's movements and mechanics. By capturing and analyzing motion data, AI can identify inefficiencies and suggest adjustments to improve performance. This scientific approach to movement is reminiscent of the precision and artistry found in ancient mythology, where heroes and gods demonstrated perfect form and technique. Through AI, athletes can refine their movements to achieve optimal efficiency and effectiveness.

In addition to wearable tech and biomechanical analysis, AI is also revolutionizing athletic gear and apparel. From smart fabrics that monitor muscle activity to AI-enhanced footwear that improves running efficiency, these innovations are transforming the way athletes train and compete. These advancements are akin to the legendary artifacts of myth, which were imbued with magical properties to aid their bearers. By integrating AI into their gear, athletes can gain a competitive edge that enhances their natural abilities.

5

Chapter 5: Strategy from the Stars

Strategizing in sports now bears the influence of celestial navigation, where AI algorithms chart the course for success. This chapter delves into the strategic applications of AI in various sports, comparing them to the guidance provided by the constellations in myth. Coaches utilize AI to devise game plans, analyze opponents, and make real-time decisions. The precision and clarity offered by these technological tools are akin to the prophetic stars that guided ancient mariners and warriors alike.

AI's role in sports strategy is multifaceted, offering coaches a wealth of information and insights that were previously inaccessible. By analyzing vast amounts of data, AI can identify patterns and trends that inform game plans and tactics. This analytical prowess is akin to the ancient practice of reading the stars to navigate and make decisions. With AI as their guide, coaches can develop strategies that maximize their team's chances of success.

One of the most significant advantages of AI in sports strategy is its ability to analyze opponents. By studying an opponent's past performances, AI can identify their strengths and weaknesses, providing valuable insights that inform game plans. This level of intelligence is reminiscent of the foresight granted by mythological seers, who could predict the actions and intentions of others. With AI's help, coaches can devise strategies that exploit their opponents' vulnerabilities while capitalizing on their own strengths.

AI also enhances decision-making during games, offering real-time analysis and recommendations. By monitoring the flow of the game and analyzing player performance, AI can suggest adjustments and substitutions that optimize the team's performance. This dynamic adaptability is akin to the guidance provided by the stars, which offered ancient navigators a reliable means of adjusting their course. With AI's assistance, coaches can make informed decisions that keep their team on the path to victory.

6

Chapter 6: The Hero's Health Journey

Health and wellness have become focal points in an athlete's career, with AI serving as the vigilant guardian. This chapter explores the role of AI in monitoring and maintaining athletes' health, likened to the protective guardianship of mythological entities. From injury prevention to recovery protocols, AI offers personalized care that echoes the nurturing touch of mythical healers like Asclepius. The narrative emphasizes how this technology ensures longevity and peak performance.

AI's role in health management is multifaceted, offering athletes a comprehensive approach to wellness. By continuously monitoring physiological metrics, AI can detect early signs of potential injuries, allowing for timely intervention. This proactive approach is akin to the vigilant guardianship of mythological protectors, who ensured the safety and well-being of their charges. Through AI, athletes can receive personalized care that addresses their unique needs and promotes long-term health.

Injury prevention is a critical aspect of an athlete's career, and AI plays a pivotal role in this area. By analyzing an athlete's biomechanics and identifying potential risk factors, AI can suggest adjustments to training routines and techniques to minimize the risk of injury. This level of precision and foresight is reminiscent of the ancient healers who could diagnose and treat ailments with divine accuracy. By leveraging AI, athletes can reduce the likelihood of injuries and maintain peak performance throughout their careers.

Recovery protocols are another area where AI's influence is profoundly felt. By monitoring an athlete's recovery process and providing personalized recommendations, AI ensures that athletes can return to peak performance levels as quickly and safely as possible. This nurturing approach is akin to the care provided by mythical healers, who possessed the knowledge and skills to restore health and vitality. Through AI, athletes can benefit from tailored recovery plans that promote optimal healing and resilience.

7

Chapter 7: Fan Engagement: A New Pantheon

The realm of fan engagement has been revolutionized, creating a new pantheon of experiences. AI-driven platforms enhance interaction, offering fans unprecedented access and immersive experiences. This chapter explores the transformation of spectators into participants, drawing parallels with ancient festivals where the lines between performer and audience were blurred. By leveraging AI, teams can create a more inclusive and engaging environment, fostering a community that mirrors the interconnectedness of mythological pantheons.

AI has transformed the way fans interact with their favorite sports and athletes, creating a more immersive and personalized experience. Through AI-driven platforms, fans can access real-time data, insights, and interactive features that enhance their connection to the game. This level of engagement is reminiscent of ancient festivals, where participants actively engaged in the celebrations and rituals. By leveraging AI, teams can create a more inclusive and engaging environment that fosters a sense of community and belonging.

One of the most significant advancements in fan engagement is the use of AI to create personalized experiences. By analyzing fan behavior and preferences, AI can tailor content and interactions to individual fans, making them feel like they are a part of the action. This level of personalization is akin to the special privileges granted to devotees in ancient mythologies, who received unique blessings and favors from their gods. Through AI, fans can enjoy a more personalized and enriching experience that deepens their connection to the sport.

AI also enhances the in-game experience for fans, offering real-time data and insights that provide a deeper understanding of the game. By integrating AI-driven analytics into broadcasts and digital platforms, fans can access detailed information about player performance, team strategies, and game dynamics. This level of insight and clarity is akin to the divine knowledge possessed by mythological figures, who could see beyond the surface and understand the underlying forces at play. Through AI, fans can gain a deeper appreciation of the game and its intricacies.

8

Chapter 8: The Alchemy of AI in Sports Economics

AI is fundamentally altering the economics of sports, akin to the alchemical pursuit of turning base metals into gold. This chapter examines the financial implications of AI in sports, from sponsorship deals to merchandising strategies. The narrative draws comparisons to mythological tales of wealth and prosperity, highlighting how AI enables smarter investments and revenue generation. It underscores the transformative power of AI, turning athletic endeavors into lucrative enterprises.

The impact of AI on sports economics is profound, offering new opportunities for revenue generation and financial growth. By analyzing market trends, consumer behavior, and sponsorship data, AI can provide valuable insights that inform business strategies and decision-making. This level of intelligence is akin to the mythical pursuit of alchemy, where practitioners sought to transform ordinary materials into valuable substances. Through AI, sports organizations can unlock new revenue streams and maximize their financial potential.

One of the most significant ways AI is transforming sports economics is through sponsorship and advertising. By analyzing data on fan engagement and demographics, AI can help organizations identify and attract potential sponsors who align with their brand and audience. This targeted approach is akin to the ancient practice of seeking divine favor and blessings to achieve prosperity. Through AI, sports organizations can secure lucrative sponsorship deals that enhance their financial stability and growth.

Merchandising strategies are another area where AI's influence is profoundly felt. By analyzing consumer behavior and preferences, AI can help organizations develop products and marketing campaigns that resonate with their audience. This level of insight and precision is reminiscent of the mythical tales of wealth and abundance, where divine intervention brought prosperity to those who sought it. Through AI, sports organizations can create successful merchandising strategies that drive sales and revenue.

9

Chapter 9: Ethical Dimensions of AI in Sports

With great power comes great responsibility, and the ethical considerations surrounding AI in sports are profound. This chapter delves into the moral quandaries posed by AI, such as data privacy, fairness, and the potential for misuse. Drawing on mythological themes of hubris and morality, the narrative explores the delicate balance that must be maintained. It underscores the importance of ethical governance to ensure that the divine gifts of AI are wielded wisely and justly.

The use of AI in sports raises important ethical questions that must be carefully considered. One of the most significant concerns is data privacy, as the collection and analysis of personal data can pose risks to athletes' privacy and security. This ethical dilemma is akin to the mythological tales of hubris, where individuals overstepped their bounds and faced dire consequences. To ensure the responsible use of AI, it is essential to establish clear guidelines and protections for data privacy.

Fairness is another critical ethical consideration, as AI has the potential to create disparities and inequalities in sports. For instance, access to advanced AI technologies may be limited to well-funded organizations, creating an uneven playing field. This ethical concern is reminiscent of the moral lessons in mythology, where the misuse of power and privilege often led to downfall.

To promote fairness and equality, it is essential to ensure that AI technologies are accessible and used in a way that benefits all athletes and teams.

The potential for misuse of AI is also a significant ethical concern, as the technology can be used to manipulate outcomes or gain unfair advantages. This ethical dilemma is akin to the mythological tales of deception and trickery, where individuals used cunning and deceit to achieve their goals. To prevent misuse, it is essential to establish ethical guidelines and oversight to ensure that AI is used responsibly and transparently in sports.

10

Chapter 10: The Future: Beyond the Horizons of Myth

As AI continues to advance, the horizon of athletic excellence expands beyond the realms of myth. This chapter speculates on future developments, envisioning a world where AI and human potential are seamlessly integrated. It draws on mythological themes of transcendence and apotheosis, suggesting that the future of sports will be characterized by unprecedented harmony between man and machine. The narrative emphasizes the boundless possibilities that await in this evolving landscape.

The future of AI in sports is filled with exciting possibilities, as advancements in technology continue to push the boundaries of what is possible. From enhanced performance analytics to innovative training methodologies, AI will play an increasingly integral role in the world of athletics. This visionary outlook is akin to the mythological themes of transcendence and apotheosis, where individuals achieved godlike status through their extraordinary feats. In the future, we can expect to see athletes achieve new levels of excellence through the seamless integration of AI.

One of the most significant future developments in AI and sports is the potential for real-time, adaptive training programs. By leveraging AI's ability to analyze data and provide instant feedback, athletes can receive personalized guidance and adjustments during their training sessions. This dynamic approach is akin to the mythological tales of divine intervention, where gods would guide and support their chosen heroes. Through AI, athletes can achieve their full potential and reach new heights of performance.

Another exciting possibility is the development of AI-driven simulations and virtual reality experiences that can enhance training and competition. By creating realistic and immersive environments, AI can provide athletes with unique opportunities to practice and refine their skills. This innovative approach is reminiscent of the mythological themes of transformation and metamorphosis, where individuals underwent profound changes to achieve greatness. Through AI, athletes can experience transformative training that prepares them for the challenges of the real world.

Real-world examples bring the intersection of AI and mythology to life, showcasing athletes who epitomize this fusion. This chapter presents case studies of modern-day heroes who have harnessed AI to achieve remarkable feats. Drawing parallels with mythological figures, the narrative highlights their journeys, triumphs, and the role of AI in their success. It serves as a testament to the transformative power of technology in the realm of sports.

One compelling case study is that of a professional soccer player who leveraged AI to enhance their performance and achieve remarkable success. By using AI-driven analytics to analyze their movements and optimize their training, this athlete was able to improve their agility, speed, and overall performance on the field. This journey is akin to the mythological tales of heroes who underwent rigorous trials and transformations to unlock their full potential. Through AI, this athlete achieved greatness and became a modern-day hero.

11

Chapter 11: The Pantheon's Legacy

The legacy of AI and mythology in sports is a testament to human ingenuity and the pursuit of excellence. This final chapter reflects on the lasting impact of this convergence, celebrating the achievements and innovations that have reshaped athletics. It draws on themes of legacy and immortality, suggesting that the contributions of AI will endure, much like the timeless tales of myth. The narrative concludes with a vision of a future where the pantheon of play continues to inspire and elevate the human spirit.

The impact of AI on the world of sports is profound and far-reaching, with advancements that have transformed the way athletes train, compete, and engage with fans. This chapter reflects on the lasting legacy of this convergence, celebrating the achievements and innovations that have reshaped the landscape of athletic excellence. By drawing on themes of legacy and immortality, we can appreciate the enduring contributions of AI and its role in shaping the future of sports.

The integration of AI into sports has created a new pantheon of excellence, where athletes can achieve extraordinary feats and push the boundaries of human potential. This legacy is reminiscent of the timeless tales of myth, where heroes and gods achieved greatness through their remarkable abilities and accomplishments. Through AI, athletes can unlock new levels of performance and achieve feats that were once considered impossible, leaving a lasting legacy for future generations to admire.

The advancements in AI and sports technology also have a profound impact on the way fans engage with their favorite sports and athletes. By creating more immersive and personalized experiences, AI has transformed the fan experience and fostered a sense of community and connection. This legacy of engagement and inclusivity is akin to the ancient festivals and rituals that brought people together to celebrate their shared passions and interests.

As we look to the future, we can envision a world where the pantheon of play continues to inspire and elevate the human spirit. The advancements in AI and sports technology will undoubtedly continue to push the boundaries of what is possible, creating new opportunities for athletes, fans, and organizations alike. This enduring legacy is a testament to the transformative power of AI and its ability to shape the future of sports in ways that are both innovative and inspiring.

In the digital age, the arenas of old have transformed into virtual coliseums, where AI facilitates and enhances athletic competitions. Esports, in particular, has seen explosive growth, driven by AI's capabilities in game design, player analytics, and fan engagement. This chapter explores how AI is revolutionizing the world of competitive gaming, drawing parallels to the grand spectacles of ancient Rome. The narrative delves into the ways AI is shaping the future of esports, creating a new era of digital gladiators.

12

Chapter 14: The Muse of Innovation

Innovation in sports technology is akin to the inspiration provided by the muses of ancient mythology. AI-driven advancements in equipment, training methodologies, and performance analytics continue to push the boundaries of what athletes can achieve. This chapter examines the role of innovation in athletic excellence, drawing comparisons to the creative inspiration provided by the muses. The narrative highlights the groundbreaking technologies and methodologies that are transforming the world of sports.

As AI becomes increasingly integrated into sports, ensuring fairness and integrity is paramount. This chapter explores the ethical considerations and challenges associated with AI in sports, drawing on themes of justice and morality from ancient mythology. The narrative delves into the efforts to maintain a level playing field, prevent cheating, and ensure that AI is used responsibly and ethically in athletic competitions. By addressing these challenges, the chapter emphasizes the importance of fair play and integrity in the modern pantheon of sports.

The stories of mythological heroes continue to inspire and motivate athletes to achieve greatness. This chapter examines the enduring influence of mythology on sports culture, drawing parallels between the trials and triumphs of ancient heroes and the challenges faced by modern athletes. By exploring the motivational power of myth, the narrative highlights the ways in which these timeless tales continue to resonate with athletes and inspire them to reach new heights.

The influence of AI and mythology in sports extends beyond individual athletes and teams, shaping the global landscape of athletic excellence. This chapter explores the international impact of AI in sports, examining how technology is bridging cultural and geographical divides. By drawing on themes of unity and interconnectedness from mythology, the narrative highlights the ways in which AI is fostering a global community of athletes, fans, and organizations. This chapter underscores the transformative power of AI in creating a more inclusive and interconnected world of sports.

The future of athletic excellence begins with the next generation of athletes. AI is revolutionizing youth sports by providing young athletes with access to advanced training methodologies, performance analytics, and personalized development programs. This chapter explores the role of AI in youth sports academies, drawing parallels to the ancient mythological schools where young heroes were trained. By leveraging AI, these academies can nurture and develop the potential of young athletes, ensuring that they grow into the champions of tomorrow.

Coaching has been transformed by AI, with intelligent systems providing coaches with valuable insights and tools to enhance their training programs. This chapter examines the role of AI as a cybernetic coach, offering real-time feedback, performance analysis, and strategic recommendations. Drawing on themes of mentorship and guidance from mythology, the narrative highlights how AI is empowering coaches to bring out the best in their athletes. By integrating AI into coaching, teams can achieve new levels of excellence and success.

The integration of AI into sports extends beyond individual athletes and teams, creating a comprehensive ecosystem that encompasses everything from training facilities to fan engagement platforms. This chapter explores the AI-driven sports ecosystem, drawing parallels to the interconnected worlds of mythology. By examining the various components of this ecosystem, the narrative highlights how AI is creating a seamless and holistic approach to athletic excellence. From smart stadiums to AI-powered analytics platforms,

CHAPTER 14: THE MUSE OF INNOVATION

this chapter underscores the transformative impact of AI on the entire sports industry.

The Pantheon of Play: How AI and Mythology Are Revolutionizing Athletic Excellence

In a world where technology and ancient tales converge, "The Pantheon of Play" takes readers on a journey through the extraordinary intersection of artificial intelligence and mythology in the realm of sports. This compelling narrative explores how AI is transforming athletic excellence, likening its impact to the divine interventions and legendary feats of mythological heroes.

From the genesis of AI in sports to the creation of a new digital coliseum, each chapter delves into different aspects of this revolutionary transformation. Readers will discover how AI acts as the modern Oracle of Delphi, providing athletes with divine-like insights and guidance. They will journey through the titanic trials of AI-driven training methodologies and explore the mythical enhancements that push the boundaries of human capability.

The book also examines the ethical dimensions of AI in sports, drawing on themes of justice and morality from ancient mythology. It highlights the challenges of maintaining fairness and integrity in an AI-enhanced world, emphasizing the importance of responsible and ethical governance.

Through captivating case studies and real-world examples, "The Pantheon of Play" showcases modern-day heroes who have harnessed AI to achieve remarkable feats. The narrative celebrates the transformative power of technology in sports, drawing parallels to the timeless tales of mythological heroes and gods.

As readers journey through the book, they will gain a deeper understanding of how AI is revolutionizing athletic excellence and shaping the future of sports. With themes of innovation, legacy, and transcendence, "The Pantheon of Play" offers a visionary outlook on the boundless possibilities that await in this evolving landscape. Whether you're a sports enthusiast, a technology aficionado, or a lover of mythology, this book promises to inspire and elevate your understanding of the modern pantheon of play.

www.ingramcontent.com/pod-product-compliance
Lightning Source LLC
LaVergne TN
LVHW020744090526
838202LV00057BA/6223